POEMS

1964 - 1980

POEMS

1964-1980

M. L. Rosenthal

New York   Oxford
OXFORD UNIVERSITY PRESS
1981

Copyright © 1981 by Oxford University Press, Inc.

Library of Congress Cataloging in Publication Data

Rosenthal, M. L. (Macha Louis), 1917–
Poems, 1964–1980.

Includes index.
I. Title.
PS3568.084P6   811'.54   81–9622
ISBN 0–19–502996–8   AACR2

Blue Boy on Skates, copyright © 1964 by Oxford University Press, Inc.
Beyond Power, copyright © 1969 by Oxford University Press, Inc.
The View from the Peacock's Tail copyright © 1972 by M. L. Rosenthal
She: A Sequence of Poems, copyright © 1977 by M. L. Rosenthal
Frontispiece for *She: A Sequence of Poems*, copyright © 1977 by Richard Pousette-Dart

Printing (last digit): 9 8 7 6 5 4 3 2 1

Printed in the United States of America

Grateful acknowledgment is made to the following publications in which many of these poems first appeared: *Agenda* (London), *American Poetry Review, American Poets in 1976* (Bobbs-Merrill Company), *Antaeus, Carleton Miscellany, The Humanist, Modern Poetry Studies, The Nation, The New Review* (London), *The New Yorker, The New York Quarterly, The New York Times, The Observer* (London), *The Ontario Review, Partisan Review, Phantomas* (Brussels), *Phylon, Poems for Shakespeare 9* (London), *Poetry* (Chicago), *Poetry Northwest, Present Tense, Quarterly Review of Literature, The Reporter, Salmagundi, Saturday Review, Shenandoah, The Spectator* (London), *Stony Brook, Sumac,* and *The Times Literary Supplement* (London).

Two of the poems were published earlier in my *Poetry and the Common Life* (Oxford University Press, 1974).

She: A Sequence of Poems was first published by BOA Editions in a limited edition.

M.L.R.

Contents

x

from
Blue Boy on Skates

(1964)

To Victoria—

translations from a language
more raucous than English,
speech of wild angels
on Eden's lost reaches
joking with dolphins
during commercials,
screech of wan centaurs
rasping rebellion
to wheel-prisoned Ixion
though he can't be listening.

Message

A message from Helen of Troy! —
    "Mack, I want you!
    Come to 88 East 88 Street at once!
    I love you! I need you!"
Helen, my darling, I can't live without you.
I'll come at once. Just give me a few hours
To find out my life-work, and to do it —
No, wait! Promise you'll wait! I can't bear
Not having you. Just let me
                  get
                      these few
Things done first. I'll be there in a jiffy.

        (SOME YEARS LATER. YOURS TRULY
        IS NOW EXACTLY NINETY-THREE
        YEARS, TEN MONTHS, OLD.)

I remember that night in Hampstead. Clear January
Air of London, heady, starry, crisp
As October in New Hampshire. Hampstead Heath:
The sweet, cold air; the hollow calls
Of waterbirds.

                    The heart
For very joy turned heavy. To think
Of love's simplicities denied, deferred, far-drifted.
Death should have come that moment!

                                      From the chilled

Sky one message!
On my hurting scalp the hair stiffened.

(HE SEARCHES THROUGH AN OLD ADDRESS-BOOK.)

I do not remember her name, her face, her city.

My Reflection in the Study Window
(for A. B. R.)

Sweeter than peace to my troubled world
My troubling loves. What limits to the eye-nerves'
Probing edge? What proof I cannot reach
Snow's cold, stone's hardness, air's indifference
For what each proves? Those Christmas lights
A field away across the winter night
Illuminate my window-forehead in three colors. I
Would find love simple. Is it the snow,
Is it the whistling air, is it the light bulbs
Where a brain should be that put from me
My own voice drifting, my night-deep eyes,
My simple thought: *I love, I love, I love?*

It Was My Best Love

It was my best love broke my nose.
A bright nosegay then quickly rose:
The bright pain, from my best love's blows.

You hardly, now, could see the break
Where love surprised me, like the Snake
That brought down Eden with one shake.

The tiniest node, or twinge, at last
Is all can mark out from the past
That bright nosegay, my love's long waste.

The Gate

I

Have I passed through the gate without knowing?
It is not so dreadful after all.
Shadows and terrors, gather around me;
I will teach you a trembling peace.

II

I did not know where I was going
Though voices sang to me of the irrevocable.
The cold stars were shining in the sad night,
And I went out searching for my son.

III

When I found him it was too late;
I had passed through the gate, without knowing.
Strange that not until tonight
Have I seen the stars in all their silence.

IV

I welcome the dead. I hope they do not care —
Love broke their backs, but so long ago.
I have joined the mists where the old ones rustle.
Father! I am no longer immortal!

V

Father! I have believed I killed you.
My soul winged blindly and left yours alone.
I did not know of the gate, my dear.
I did not know. I did not know.

Three Conversations

I

for E. R.

I was thinking how the hunters will come to the shelters;
They'll have war-heroes' hands, smelling of raw meat.
They'll brain the babies and take the canned salmon.
Then I remembered the smell of strawberries in Jónava.

That's what you told me once — that when you were a girl,
In Jónava, the smell of strawberries filled the countryside.
When you were a girl! O happy Jews wandering
Sober among strawberries, everywhere in Jónava.

II

for E. C.

My friend, we sat on a park bench and talked of Cuba:
How deftly, so deftly, the rulers had nigh undone us,
Then, "with consummate skill," had canceled the consummation.
It was a cold week when Khrushchev tiptoed consummately off—
"Ain't nobody here but us chickens, Mr. Jack!"
If only Bertrand Russell hadn't threatened us with annihilation
All would have been well. He scared *me* into submission.

Oh, a cold, sunny day in Washington Square,
And a delegation of pot-hunting dandies was there
With two lovely, green-lidded girls (strangers to open air).
And the cop, shoving the drunk, was on his own kind of tear.
Superb were the tableaux on Washington Square.

III
for V. H. R.

When the Christian martyrs were burned, we agreed,
Anonymous Jews were used for kindling.
Do you remember that evening, staring into the river?

It was after that play of Sholem Aleichem's
Breathed Jónava strawberries into the Chicago night —
And we'd nothing to do but talk and make love.
The full moon had risen, with a mustache like Hitler's.

A Spark from Pasternak

Sweet energy of springing black boughs,

                                           "Japanese"

Against brightening blue.

                              Noon

Will burn upon us, my dear, before we rise.

Sly evergreen
Is striding in the winter woods!

Jim Dandy

He diddled the ivory keys.
He babbled in Chimpanzese.
    He dabbled in honey
    And made big money
And gave it all back to the bees.

He twirled a gay guitar.
He smoked the sweetest cigar.
    He lay on the grass
    With the head of the class
And left her all ajar.

He piped once down your lane.
He warbled a randy refrain.
    He plucked a flower
    From your mama's bower
And rode off on a golden cane.

The Tenth One

The tenth one was a diver, the thin blade,
Could cut through your neck, you'd never notice the line.
He shinnied right up, three feet over the diving board,
And circled three times, like the sword of Mahomet
(The air didn't budge, the swish being so subtle),
Then shot through the air, a glider, and then
Curved into the water, a flying parabola,
Whistled right through while the water was waiting,
Came out at Nanking!

              'Twas he, dears, that saved
The wealth of the West from the tooth of the Nippon!
'Twas he that sliced through the Japanese army!
The Mikado's men would be mooching there yet
Were't not for the tenth one, the diver, the thin blade.
They tried forward march, when he had gone through them,
And their legs went ahead, but the torsoes just floated;
'Twas then that the Nipponese army lost face!

The other nine were stout fellows, no divers.
Tradesmen they were, knew nothing of battle.
But he was the great one, the thin one, the diver.

The Intruders

A man came from a certain far place (downstairs).
Saying that the people there were dying.
The man was wearing the shoes of that place
And spoke in the accent of one that lived there;
But his shoes were torn and covered with mud,
And the man was unshaven.

Now I was sitting in my room full of charts,
Staring from my window observing my flies,
And filing my nail-files.
And here was this man, without credentials,
Breathing in my face, his hands on my desktop —
Morever, he had forgotten to remove his hat.

I put a bullet through his head.

Now here's the point: his countrymen lately
Keep setting fire to my house. One, in fact,
Who should know better (we just gave him amnesty,
After seven years in prison for marrying
My bastard daughter), touched a match to my hair
Only this morning, after serving the coffee.

One's always having one's personal affairs intruded on.

Blue Boy on Skates (Twilight)
(for L. G. R.)

Little circle
big circle
here comes a little animal on tiny wheels

> *the metal on the stone*
> *does the singing*

Look at the ghost girls whispering on the stoops

I spin and spin
until I feel them stare
and then I whirr away through the summer air

> *the metal does the ringing*
> *on the stone*

They think I live on bees and poison ivy.

To the Shades of Old-Time Révolutionnaires

Bearers forever of banners,
Marchers forever where only
The strongest can hold from their weeping:
The army of the dull and lonely;

Commanders of brooding divisions,
True to commands never heard:
"Be of the bone and the marrow
And you will remember the word."

Résumé

(In Memoriam, T. R., Jr.)

I said to my old teacher,
"I was just a child.
That's why I was wild."

I said to my old mother,
"Mother, I was right
Though you have won the fight."

I said to my old girl,
"It's lucky we lay
Then, that way."

I said to my old self,
"Throw away those shoes."
Now, there's nothing to lose.

Proverbial

In the country of seeing-eye dogs
    The blind man is king,
        The one-eyed's prime minister,
           The two-eyed's a traitor —
         Or a seeing-eye dog.

The Ideal Poet

The ideal poet's tall and gaunt,

                       agreed.

But is that ideal poet

                 syphilitic, too?

Or is he pure and rosy-cheeked? (Cries

Of: "Syphilitic!" "No! pure and rosy-cheeked!")

I say

        he's neither, or a bit of both:

Healthy, yet impure;

                 pure, yet mottled;

                            un-

mottled, yet speckled. Ra-hosy-cheeked

But with jec-yust

            the slee-ightest touch

Of the old (as I was saying) spirochete. Bring on

The penicillin, Doc.

                   The Muse

Is still a whore for a' that, an' a' that.

Liston Cows Patterson and Knocks Him Silly

I

The giant is champ of the world.
There are no heroes. In body's domination
History reveals itself without comment.

Now you are quiet. You have lighted
Your pipe. You have perused the magazines, etc.
Why not stand up, go forth, and put things right?
Mr. Liston's fists.

Mr. Patterson's, for that matter.
All militancy makes for murder.
All acquiescence makes for murder.

II

In the shallows of the mind
Are mirrored body's deeps.

III

"He can run but he can't hide." Thus spake
Joe Louis. Ironies of the warriors!

What am I doing out here in No Man's Land, anyway?
In the planet where I come from, stranger,
The matter to hand is of other things.

NO!
   LET'S HAVE VIOLENCE!
COME ON, YOU BASTARDS, I WANT TO LIVE FOREVER!
POETS, TO ARMS!
     CALL UP SOME GIRLS!
SNUB EACH OTHER IN TAVERNS!
LET ALL REVIEWS BE MERCILESS HENCEFORTH!
INTELLECTUALS, CITE YOUR SOURCES!
THERE'S NOT A MOMENT TO LOSE!

IV

She walks in beauty, in that one sweater and skirt
That are all she has. Her face is sad, sweet, round,
And scarred. Promiscuous, fastidious, and has said
She loves me. I touch. She touches. Oh,
We dance out the soiled window to the street below.
I have been turning in the air forever, I think
I may be that air, that window, that truck
That is leaping toward her on the street.
The window stares down idly at the scream.

Such a dirty street! So many old women!
Oh, they're sweeping up the pieces of a plastic doll.
She is lying on the divan again. We might be touching.
Shall I make that final turn? To her again?

Some champ has just taken away the Muse's bike
And filled her bathtub with his old clothes.
He straddles her on the divan, unglues the plastic pieces.
I can't see anything through my own soiled glass.

In a Hotel Bed

In a hotel bed, the shower-thing dripping,
Black devils bumping outside the panes softly, and corpses
Dragging down corridors to laundry chutes —

Ah, my elastic heart starts pumping in reverse;
My sprung brain beats a tom-tom on the backs of my eyeballs;
No fear I'll be asleep when the Birchers smash down my door!

When My Desire

When my desire, unknown to me,
Pierced your desire, unknown to you,
I saw you waken in the crowded room.
Power sickened us. We both turned away.
Better be blind than this kind of seeing fools.

Song

Days and nights will not retain
With dust, old leaves, or even pain

Mouth-sweetness and the curious tongue
And cunnycombs by pity stung.

Our sex let cleave, yet eyes must meet
Love's other face, as in retreat,

Prophetic gull of time that grieves
For dust, old pain, a few dead leaves.

The Old Yank

The old Yank returning home after a year in Yurrup
Wasn't telling much. He wasn't giving it away.
"Like it over there?" — "Yup."
"Glad to be back?" — "Yup."
"Give us the facts." — "Well,
They got
        statchers in Florence,
They got
        Paree (in France),
They got
        beer some places, and that
                ain't all they got."

That's all he'd say. A man
With a passport, and playing his yups close to his chest.

N. Y. Provincial

I
TUCSON, ARIZONA

It's a desert.

       It's a desert.

              It's a desert.

And it's *in* a desert.

II
HAMMOND, INDIANA

Horrible Hammond, Indiana,
More horrible than Passaic, New Jersey,
I pity you your hateful landscape,
I pity you your hideous houses,
I pity you your hamstrung inhabitants,
Dreadful Hammond, Indiana.

III
NEW YORK, NEW YORK

Jimmy Durante said it:
It's da heartada woild!

Proletarian Pastorales
(Drayman's and Carter's Division)

AUBADE

The rising sun,
      with drowsy glance,
      pulls on his pants,
gets up, and goes to work.

NOCTURNE

The setting sun,
      with parting glance,
      pulls off his pants,
lies down, and goes to sleep.

The Enemy

The enemy's a little pale guy, squats
Behind the breadbox outside the corner grocery
White-hot, for gentlest Jesus' sake,

                            angrier than the Saviour's blood

That by us Jewish kids was spilled
On Easter Sunday back in Warsaw once
When He, good priest, was sprinkling water 'round
Upon the matted heads of all His poor,
Too kind to see us Judas-smiling dandies inch
Toward His worn cassock ever closer....

Ah, Jewish kid! come forth! come forth!
I Raymond and my three staunch Christian friends
Stanley, and John, and Ignatz, do declare
That you shall not escape our holy wrath
Until you have given us the loaf of bread
And thirteen cents that you now carry!

Proud schoolboy enemies, how we fought that day.
My bread was smashed and blackened, my coins lost in the mud.
Pale Raymond, here are milk-white loaves
And sparkling pennies (could I now unmake the years)
And a free round-trip, with all expenses paid,
Back through the immortal past.
                              Oh, could enemies but crucify
Not Jesus Saviour, not Judas, not (Raymond) you or me
But sick Memory herself,
                              but foolish History!

"If I Forget Thee..."

I

Honor the poised sword of man's misery; the faces
of the mothers; the cobblestones
on which men walk to war and no fortune.

Honor not that light, cold light from an unknown star,
light that affirms nor denies, falling across fields,
whiting the stones, whetting the wind.

Curve of the comet, or peal of distant sound,
or friend who can no longer turn to me:
take me not, carry me not, show me no light of star.

For if you do, no rest;
and if I go, no return;
and if I follow, no forgiving.

II

This is that light, cold light from an unknown star,
light that affirms nor denies, falling across fields,
whiting the stones, whetting the wind.

It strikes through the darkened trees, the silent bar,
seeking the naked mist, the membrane of life.

III

Curve of the comet, or peal of distant sound,
or friend who can no longer turn to me:

and if I stay, skull and coffin, three, four;
and if I follow, white unanswering light,
light forever, white and no return.

Memorial Day Inscription

Streets where the moral man
Can hold death waiting:
I long to see you, pace your honored stones,
Dream on the faces of your living throngs.

from
Beyond Power

(1969)

Reality, the Void Abandoned by Imagination

I

Springing with white blossoms
                    those trees, bright the air
and that fountain, aureole spray, love's essence, dancing there
ravished by bullfrogs' chanting—
                    they neither know nor care
that we are leaving, now, we and our marvelous affair.

II

Heavy with May, this air,
these trees. They do not care . . .
The fountain waits, not for us, and will wait
after we've left.

            And the frogs, passionate,
forgot to ask for our permission . . .
                        Nowhere
came we, no color left in this garden, here,
                        we and our marvelous affair.

Into the Mirror

Love's a mirror where we see
not ourselves but another, who does not see
                                    (perhaps)
out from the unground center of the glass.

                                 Through
Norfolk's flat fields this train
                    carries me.
                       Planes
of green, racing from everywhere, fly past.
                             It is
the actual, the present, hard as glass,
                      that's flying past.

Were I to smash
                  against the flying world, I should be
inside the mirror.   Your wanting eyes
would splinter, and would enter me.

                           I have been
where the thrust of all our planes within
                      your spinning world
set the whole
           past flying —
                blind thrust
into your dreaming center.

But now,

and awake, and here,

           Norfolk's green world out there flying,

it is a love-thrust takes me

           into, out of, nothing.

Were I to smash

        against that flying mirror,

                it would pierce

me with your waiting eyes.

          And I have touched

that wound already, where you're poised

            waiting

                to return,

                    my love,

to return

      into me

        your love

           to me.

Love Wrapped Me in Darkness
(adapted from the Urdu of Sajjad Baqir Rizvi)

Love wrapped me in darkness, gathering like a cloud,
Then filled my eyes with fountains of moonlight.

She before whom my desire had lain speechless
Then woke my full song;

Whose eyes all others watched for in secret
Sought mine alone, to bless with her light;

Who touched the air with her breath of flowers
Was snared by her own song, that I made for her.

Gazelle, mistrusting even your shadow,
You faced bravely around and into my arms.

Stare into your mirror!
My desire is singing in the curve of your mouth;

And these wandering lines and couplets
Came forth in desire, became your poem.

BAQIR made these rhythms
Who thought himself helpless, once, and joyless.

Just When I'd Hardened My Soul

I

Just when I'd hardened my soul,
the girl remembered her loneliness.

Knives dancing about my head!   But I
am graced, of late, by her forgetfulness.

II

"Psyche my soul"
remembers her loneliness.

Her knives dance
about my head!

She needs my death!   But she
disdains to wake that loneliness.

Returning

Waiting to be with you again

For we are launched, love, through that arc
Of flowering life, where all journeys meet

Arc of the world, of all our moments self by self
And of the world's splintered moments, stabbing, bringing the blood

We in flowering space, having found our arc

Love Song

Written in the sky: birds, clouds, blue.
Spoken by silence: they cannot help
being beautiful.

You cannot help being beautiful, and we must love
the sculptured flow of all that's secretive;
must love the embroidered band about your hair.
And though you do not dream as we dream
you feel yourself unbud before us, bare.

O thou too dear for my possessing . . .

> A lion glares through the autumn leaves.
> Darker crouches God's devouring blue.
> Gold eyes lost amid the speeding stars.

Love me, my love, love me.
                            These hands have turned to petals,
this whole body blossomed to find the full
of our divine and double, fructifying solitude.

You cannot help being beautiful.
                            You come
to withhold our kisses from our graves.

Love in the Luncheonette

Five deadpan Americans sitting along a counter:
The good blonde girl pours their morning coffee deadpan.
From the deadpan radio
                    Flamenco passion pours,
                    And then the desolate melody
                    From the profitable French film of childhood betrayal.

"Marry me, blonde!" (It's the electric fan talking.) "I'll cool you and skin
                                                                    you!"
"Marry *us*!" (It's the seven empty counter stools.) "We'll spin you and
                                                                    spin you!"
"Marry *me*!" (It's the cash-register now.) —
                    "*Chin-n-ng!* I adore you!"

The coffee's dying of loving, it's turning lukewarmer.
The catsup's done bleeding, now it's clotting.
The five wax Americans melt through the doorway, into sultry August.

The good blonde girl drops on a sighing stool, and spins.
Someone else's bosom rams by, outside the plateglass window. —
                    Chin-n-ng! I adore you! —
Above it a pug-dog mug, below it a swaying eggplant . . . Could *you*
Design such a woman? Such *two* women?

"O, my blonde!" (That's me, tracked down in my lovelorn booth.)
The radio's got "Vietnam" stuck in its deadpan throat.
Turn it off! Turn it on! Get the proprietor quick!

Pope Paul has just dropped the word, fortunately in translation.
He says we should love one another. I do! I do! I do!
        Chin-n-ng! Adore I do you!

Sussex: The Downs

High grass. Sun. Nothing else, anywhere.

I, a solid space in high grass under the sun.

Reality, you never abandoned me. I have you, here.

Intractable beings—who?—
slipping, touching, needing, leaving
into, out of, where?
                    Let the sun beat down.

                                    We'll pity Arabs,
run guns for the Irgun,
rise in arcs of rainbow penetration from one soul's height to another's,
reach, lose, in the high hot grass,
blood-keen as Satan's armies marching,
sparkling, perfect, as God's armies marching,
throwing our bodies in front of the tanks,
plowing our tanks over bodies thrown in our way.

            To hold the lead is hard;
            to find the inner track fatal; so
                    let the race founder in the grass.

While we lie on the heights of the Downs
may green and gold prevail!
Warmth be the banner above us
and, if we sit up,

          let there be cows in the dale!

Beyond Power

I

PARIS, *1968*

Banners surge red and black! *Vive la fraternité*!

Where the new voice touches
leap of the forgotten heart

Fed

by tributary infinities a flood of spectres,
waving sparklers, limps, leaps, prances,
sways faint with laughter. Songs in all languages!

Toothless masks

are shed. The secret faces show, young and beautiful.

Cowardice a lost art
Death a lost art

Spilt blood on paving stones calls back
the brute wash of ancient powers . . .
Scuttle of killers down tunnels and sewers . . .
Blasted are the meek for their leaders inherit the earth.

Opposite the red-fanged blaze of northern sun
see the ghost-moon now, in clear daylight,
riding the southern sky.
It holds up, over a cloud of furious gray;
behind it a cloud of radiant white.

II

BEYOND POWER

Darkness lowers over the great wooded park.
The deer close toward us; the trees heave grim and massive.
Chilled lovers shiver now with the coming of dusk.
The deer and the tree-trunks are drifting nearer.

Inside my head an ancient city whirls
that a god once touched and, absentmindedly, destroyed.
The river of our dreams carries us where we willed to be.
The darkness touches us. I put out my hand to you.

Death's beautiful dandy I would be, my speech beating
with the pure pulse of lovers in their sudden dream.
Where the new voice touches, leap of the forgotten heart—
the darkness whelms over us, and the river of our dreams.

To the Rulers
(to lay down arms)

I

This imperial day the dawnsun calls,
quick shadow like the meridian line unseen,
calls with unheard voice through afternoon's
bright arcade, calls after the bright lord
whose golden, purposed path leads down
to voluptuous dark boudoirs in the dead man's land.

II

Do not speak of Auschwitz, or even Vietnam.
The ass's skull is braying again:
Some day, science will put everything right.
Slam the face shut, quick-freeze the heart;
our true loves have all died in our arms.

III

Lay down arms.

> What bomb unmakes
> the unblinking past?
> What honor (say
> what you will) awakes
> the napalmed babe?

Consider the dead

> of the East, of the West.
> Rulers,
> fear ye not?

He who is right

      stays his hand.
      Lo, the poor addict
      fears withdrawal.
      Fear ye not.

A Dream of Mayakovsky's Suicide Note

Ineffable, slapstick despair of dreams.
The phone rings. Sam Middlebrook's voice.
"The coat is all right, the vest is all right, but Sam"—
(*You're* Sam! *I'm* Mack.)—"Sam, you made the pants too long."
My heart breaks.

Don't never go out with no plumbers, girls.
They're always forgettin' their tools.
And, boys,
don't never outwit no gods, promise?
An even worse fate (if I could remember) awaits you.

"Goodbye,
I hope this won't harm any of you. It's just
this old baby-grief. Thought it was nobody's
grief but my own. Nothing, really. And

'ONE THROW OF THE DICE'
will never change all that.—Or just *this* throw can.
And, baby, here goes. How long does it take?
Depends.

I don't recommend it for others."

I Strike a Match . . .

My mind's still the mirror of your death.
I strike a match; the flame's reflected
huger than I'd have thought in the breathless window-air.

The electric clock's still ticking.
The neighbor's car burns behind the reflected glare
in the inert world blazing and blown by the wind out there
where the monster Death's plying the storms of autumn
and the men and women tick off their minutes so carelessly

superb! Mother, I was driving
down the highway last night —
you know, the one our road runs into . . .
A towering man in a trenchcoat stood at the side,
his back toward me, as if surveying all blackness.
Then he turned, to glare into the glare of my headlights,
his glowing skull, his bone jack-o'-lantern smile.
Then my second-sight ended: A towering road-sign cried
DANGER!

It is November now.
It was August when you left us, dying
from the dangerous world into the mirror of our dreaming.

Winter without Danny

Snow, snow, serious snow.

On my brother's grave, the serious snow.

Bearded old ladies, coiffured college boys,
Unorthodox Jews, Orthodox Goys,
stumble, tumble, to this pedantry of snow.

Sweeties in your nighties, you may tremble and glow
by your heart-shaped windows —

the bright world's all snow.

"To Think of Time"

At long last, this heart
stiller than this city
content within this body
parting with one lost beat
from all this that it loves.

Angels

Angels, are you still old and portly?
Do you still follow your salt-free diets?
Do you plan long trips through Paradise because "it's such a beautiful
country"?

And God, do Your old friends still lug their shopping bags full of
ruined causes?
Do they still crack jokes about their arthritis?
Do they favor You with the delicious sayings of their grandchildren?

Angels, do you stare down now pitying the soldiers and the scared
cities?
Do you still pray in fear for the lovely young, all so bright?
Do you never doubt even now that they will surely do right?

Death comes unexpected, even to old ambassadors from Paradise.
Just one surprise of pain more, another sudden fall, but then the
recognition.
(Oh, it's all right. Life was interesting. This is the recall.)

Who forced You, God, to let them grow old
before You wired them their wings? If they'd got them in time
they'd still have used motels, maybe, but wouldn't have needed the car.

America and cortisone are so beautiful and expensive!
They never wanted to take help from anyone, even You,
but I do wish You'd fastened on wings for their mission.

Farewell
(to E. F. R., 1893-1967)

By your window,
writing your gay letters,
in love with the great elm's leaves—
my soul! my happiness! real as a pillow.
Time put her arms around you, and you slept on her breast.

from
*The View from
the Peacock's Tail*

(1972)

Like Morning Light

(An inscription for Eva E., 1918-1936, whom I knew as a child in Passaic, N. J.)

Russians, Poles, Jews—all die in this late November rain.
Outdoors, indoors, the same death-draught penetrates
whatever's only matter. Here in my head
the rain wanders, the clock unwinds, and the brave beam
of my desklamp grows duskily misty, revealing and hiding you.

Two children together, telling each other poems. If from your early
grave, you rose again now, onto the real streets, a real woman alive,
eyes still like myopic diamond knives vaguely piercing the mists,
a slight, sultry princess-slave slipping frailly amid the peasantry,
would I know the child I once saw in her bath and thought it music?
Yet you linger. Around you the stench of the Botany Mills and the
stagnant Passaic.

You linger
gently, gaily, ignorant you are dying,
like the morning light over the Mount of Olives.

As all the bright children linger on the world's poisoned streets.

from *His Present Discontents: A Sequence*

I

TO HIS OTHER SPIRIT

"There comes over me some days a feeling, abundant, political . . ." (Vallejo)

I know you so well, not at all, beloved
apple of my bough, heart's-thorn, wise little spirit
who will outlive me, and my fear for you, and yours
for me in the world's wide room where through all my weathers
I move, walk, ride, dream in my pants like Einstein's or
Lenin's, full of the latest wrinkles at seat or knee,
posh as somebody's grandpa darkening on an old daguerreotype.

"We are transmitters," Lawrence said, but you will rise
on an arc of your own nature, beautiful, beyond even yourself—
who knows what it will be like then? Does not every life,
every painting, poem dance out the grief of beauty and joy?
"There comes over me some days a feeling, abundant, political," when I
                                            think of you
(floating forever, as you know, in my own amniotic soul
where something of you took form, mother to myself as well) . . .
stormy, volatile, tentative as all living thought. But you have been born
and will be again, airy creature—myself, and far from me.

On a bed, shooting up with your hepatitopoeic needles,
"fuck" and "shit" on the tip of your tongue's pride, music
of wrathful vileness, time dripping away
from the crusted corners of your seraph's-eyes while
the retch-stale air of your closed-chamber dreams

sucks in the drowsy host of sullen flies, friends
settling in, companionable death-row prison-mates,
and the invisible sun and stars and moon
swing overhead singing death's immortal sway—

and the earth, they say, swings 'round the sun,
the days become the seasons, the seasons the years,
and we in our ignorance swaying our plumed and cocked bodies
while time grows crystal in the soul. You have arisen
from your grimy couch, opened your brilliant eyes, put sighing
aside the womb-bliss of needles, and wavered forth.
Dawn waits, still unseen, but the richest suns, sometimes,
spill through the sullied winter-sky. And the clear
dance of thought, grateful as a flogged puppy, resumes
and the charmed charnel fountain-play of poems, midwinter spring indeed!

Oh, I could speak Chinese, perceive how doorbells work,
lead bloodless revolutions skipping through the parks, roll
the whole dismantled creation into one gentle poem, bouncing like a ball
for children to throw and old men glaze with their grateful tears.
The skulls of Kiev, Oswiecim, Songmy, Gettysburg
will thunder underground toward the tenpins of Jerusalem
and on the Day of Judgment rocket upwards chanting
of the miracle that was life, that dreamed to walk on water,
that swallowed all that was, and then was not.

II
AM I THAT DANCER?

This very dusk, intangible velvet,
my fingers are walking through you, my eyes listen,
you have taken me at one touch, I dance on your rooftops—

Am I that dancer now, whom once I saw
top-hatted, gloved, in evening pumps,
footing it swiftly, an inch above Fifth Avenue,
dream-dandy flitting toward unimaginable gaiety
like the thought of joy skimming among gravestones?

His shoes had tiny wings of light.
He paused at the corner for the traffic to pass,
then sparkled across the street and was gone.

III

WORKING

Working slowly, your way, through the air
working slowly, into your own brain's maze
if that's the way it works
till you've worked it through

Still, still, it won't work
You'll never work it out
You'll never work around it

It's, just, dead, center.

Work it up and out, the dead stump?
It, just, happens, to
be you.

VIOLENCE

Poets of Bengal, the wash of the great sea-stench
must, at last, seal even your tongues and ears.
The clamorous life-stench, we see now, was but
the overture breathed by man's genius to the end of this silence.

The killer has balls and a belly, like mine.
The soles of his feet sweat, like mine.
I'm in a hardening world inside, like his.
The world's full of my kills. I've every
weaker man in my helpless grasp, like him.

I can't sort myself out from this great tidal wave,
millions drowning under millions, till all men are silent at last.

Like a wave breaking around, but not over, beauty's solitude,
my own surging halts at the tide-line, then hurries back over hissing sands,
and I learn it was not fear of violence but my own sure forgetting—
it was not conquest my own solitude sought, but to break in waves about
beauty—
that made the wave of my yearning to leap like a squadron of lancers,
then silently drop
away again, from that marble image on the hissing sands.

V

CRUELTY

As I walk down a city street, a knot of children are playing about the front stairway of an old wooden house. Suddenly a girl of ten, lean, bitter, kicks the shin of a five-year-old boy with all her might. He falls whimpering to the sidewalk. I stop to remonstrate with the girl or comfort the boy—it is confusing—and adult faces, cursing me, explode at the windows.

I remember another time. My wife had taken our baby son to a city playground. A little girl there (she might have been the same one) walked up and slapped his face sharply. Absolutely impersonal.

And further back, when my younger brother and I were both small children. One day he came home screaming. Some boys had tied a cord around his genitals, a fact we did not discover at once.

Sometimes, when I am dismayed by the rudeness or the violence of the young, I recall the suave, smiling cruelties of those in power, how they use their own authority, and "the rules," and even their knowledge and wisdom, to break the hopes of others. Then the rudeness or violence of the young seems touching!—an inarticulate response forced on them to their disadvantage, including that great disadvantage of feeling in the wrong. But I must remember, too, that cruelty of every sort has its own laws, not to be explained away.

VI

SCORPIONS

My beautiful young friends are aging gracefully now.
Soon they will be twinkling old gentlemen and ladies.
We never shout at each other now when we meet.
We are always delighted with each other now when we meet.

Once we prowled like panthers, or skunks, in each other's lairs.
We laughed too much, or we bristled, under each other's magic.
Sexual heat, tropic steam, misted our vision.
Impaled on our own nobility, we thought our passions depraved.

Sedately at family dinner, we devoured our prettier cousins,
raping them and our younger aunts at half-past the soup.
Hard, proud as our bodies, we accepted the bounty
of our elders (their lives) indifferently, after a quarrel.

Some of us actually died, or were actually killed; some actually did kill.
Blood leaked terror over us, staining our monstrous regiment.
What were we? What are we? Sentimental scorpions?
Yes, just like old Yahweh, in whose image we were cast.

VII

"TO BODIES GONE": PYGMALION REMEMBERING

"See, how everything opens out; thus do we . . ." (Rilke)

Worlds of ivory nakedness . . . faces smiling and Chinese under tossing hair, the painted marble eyes fixed on some distant inward prospect. Incredible frail, silken shoulders, narrow, blushing breasts, and that ludicrously simple, cartoonist's slash that conceals world within world within world, itself only just not concealed by the frond of sweet maidenhair . . . the face and body of anonymous, amazing womanliness, insistent on itself, its uniqueness, its name and station as are the waves that come storming towards the shore to shock and engulf us forever, here, now, where everything flowers in one moment.

Rising and falling astride me, terribly intent. The eyes now bright, with pupils dilated, and now tightly clenched. That pale, self-enclosed face going completely inward. The delicate stalk of body swaying and rocking over the slender, mobile, yet still marble thighs. The breasts still marble, rigid, yet swaying, the painted nipples actually hot! Pausing for one endless moment, eyes staring, seeing and unseeing, here and gone on the hissing Cyprian sands.

VIII

BALANCING

on   both   hands

emptiness

DOWN   DOWN
comes   comes
the   the
one   other
handful

the whole

weight   of   space!

How Much Experience Do We Need?

one slow full rich oblivion of loving
one sharp stab of death

        enough for a lifetime and a deathtime

        why so many
        seasons and days
        newspapers spilling over

when even
forsythia and daffodils
or one quick yellow-shafted flicker's return
can chill without warning?

Schlaflied

Einmal, wenn ich dich verlier,
wirst du schlafen können, ohne
dass ich wie eine Lindenkrone
mich verflüstre über dir?

Ohne dass ich hier wache und
Worte, beinah wie Augenlider,
auf deine Brüste, auf deine Glieder
niederlege, auf deinen Mund?

Ohne dass ich dich verschliess
und dich allein mit Deinem lasse,
wie einen Garten mit einer Masse
von Melissen und Sternanis?

— Rainer Maria Rilke

Lullaby

(after Rilke's "Schlaflied")

Some day, when I lose you,
will you be able to sleep then,
without my whispering, like a crown of linden
rustling into silence, above you?

Without my watching here, without
my words, soft as eyelids almost,
brushing down on your breasts, on your limbs
gently, and on your lips?

Without my leaving you, eased,
folded shut within yourself at last
like a garden, a mass
of melissas and star-anise?

First Rilke Variation
("Einmal, wenn ich dich verlier")

Some day, when I lose you,
I'll think how lightly
the days came and went while
I was finding you.

The days opened on you:
the light touched you so gently—
secret aureole
cradling your moments.

Late at Night

Peering out into the dark
gets you your face thrown right back at you
through the window-pane.

Everything flings back
out of the dark into the light of yourself—
ennui of unprejudiced thought.

Do you know the little zoo
in Golders Hill Park—
the peacocks there?

Feathered Orients,
sheen of metallic blaze and blue
and those all but invisible heads, almost intaglio,

one-dimensional,
murderous, perhaps, if they struck,
pressed into their glittering, turning shields.

Lo, how he turns,
hoping for the peahen's best
(if he notices when it happens)

endlessly patient—and suddenly
the Maharajah of Dacca
has his back to me!

I'm backstage!
O unrehearsed rear of the Real,
the view from the peacock's tail!

Everything gone brown-grey, barnyard-homey,
and all that proud shield of glory up front
flung into his audience from what's back here.

Yes, Achilles behind *his* shield, just stricken,
must have seen himself all the way back here
where everything *really* happens.

Here's where the claws touch earth.
Here's whence the peahen's trodden.
Here the dropping, all that's vulnerable, all the damned tautology—

great, outspread, oppressive wings of the commonplace,
towering above, behind us,
shriek of the chaotic, denying glory!

I turned my burning shield toward you,
and you, yours, to me.
Did we see, through the reflections, some glimmer

of one real another, standing
back here, back there, peering
into the darkness between?

To think that I wanted
to pierce back through your eyes
into the brain, the being, the worlds around "you"!

Can I touch the world without treading it?
Know the suffering without redoubling it?
Love without hunching the whole of my peacock's back along?

Notations of Love

I

YOUR PASSION PLEASES ME

It pleases me. There's
a white dusty car, a white cloud, a mid-March wind
all rushing past. Swallows, flying leaves, shadows left
from the dead winter's last late afternoon. Wild ducks
are flying by. I want
to meet you suddenly on the street
coming to me out of the brightest, blue-
est sky, almost terrible.

Come flying on this wind!

II

INCREDULOUS, OUR BODIES ARE REMEMBERING

Incredulous, our bodies are remembering.
Our loins are heavy, remembering
the sweet penetration, holding it.
It holds, strange distant perfume
in the cold and champagne air:
ourselves, we, essence of us
far away and present to our inner touch.

III

IN THE BURNING GLASS—

at the pinpoint of flame, where flesh
concenters all unceasing, hurling, driven spirit
in the marriage bed of our love, there bursts
before our dismayed ecstasy
the terrible human face of need—

the dead face longing to return,
face of the swollen-bellied babe with heavy-drooping eyelids.

IV

FIRST MORNING OF JANUARY

First morning of January: brilliant cold smile of this new year.
My love and I woke together, warm and smiling.
A mid-March wind had carried the months away.
Now this first wind of the new year
whirls back out of the West
bringing the old months home.

Your passion pleases me. I fear the passion that kills.

Love, come flying on the wind
as when the beast's eyes first opened wide and he saw
in the brightest, bluest sky the depths
and sweep of desire.

Each Day Beats Down

Each day beats down upon
this staunchest flower
in any garden, that ever
in any weather
bloomed at the whirlwind's center.

A sudden joy. Golden
petals open. This one
dizzy bee finds this storied
uncompromising glory.

Theater Talk

The audience dreams in the dark. The keen images
leap from a dead man's mind to the bright-lit stage
answering unasked questions with their flashing unanswered ones.

> *"Why, that's my dainty Ariel: I shall miss thee."*

We dream in the dark. The voices
hold in the suddenly stilled air.
The lights disperse the audience.
The keen images have leapt from the emptying room.

"Master, I have returned. I have missed thee, master."

—Or so I dreamt, in the dark,
of that master, still dreaming in his clasp of darkness,
who struck those images into glowing air. And
they return, streaming back to him with love . . .
No. No return. Only the flashing moment on the stage:
> *"Was't well done?"*
> *"Bravely, my diligence,—thou shalt be free."*

Geometries of Haifa: Night

The full moon explodes over the city—
and thrusts a glittering blade far over the sea.

     "We labor like pistons here."
     "It's dull."
     "Barbed wire encloses the full heart's garden here."

Arc of the moon and three stars over Haifa,
arc of the lights of Haifa below,
and the swordthrust of the full moon over the flat black sea.

My Friend's Anger

My friend is angry. He'd kill
those butcher-buffoons screwing all the nations—
betrayers of all the languages—
and even their bleating victims for being too damned dumb
to feel the shame when they get shafted.

His anger refuses to rest.
He quarrels with the very air for its indifference.
And with his own acquiescence—he earns a wage,
loves a girl, like every traitor
to honest poverty and the great human cause.

We want! to taste the snow, hear sweet words of pure thought, love
like angels who awoke this morning to find ourselves men.
"They" won't let us.
I too want to kill them
if their sodden lives could ever be restored.

We dwell within these tiny skulls.
We're primitives, we suck our charnel comforts.
The guts bulge through the transparency of our "minds."
Once and for all, to love the tentativeness of sweet thought
and to divide—share—our bread, love, souls, labors!

Seniority, or It Stands to Reason

These autumn leaves, with their gold or crimson sheen,
could hardly recommend the fresh young green
spring leaves for mature responsibilities.
You need *experience* to capture sun for trees.

Deaths of the Poets

Take the voices away
that pierce the always waiting ear,
splinters of God, biblical shell-fragments, screams
of police-sirens and out of the mouths
of dead faces holding steady in the mind's endless galleries—
voices that return and return and return.

Don't come too close.
I want to lift off.
I want to penetrate you. Don't you penetrate me.
I want to lift off from the red-hot ground
with my load of three-point-five billion passengers, my load
of three-point-five billion passengers screaming in here.

Touch a magnet, maybe I'll become one.
The ground's red-hot, and the sky,
and the air. They're jumping in front of the trucks
and from the bridges. They're shoving
their beautiful heads in the gas-ovens. They're
listening, listening, can't stop listening.

Touch a magnet, maybe I'll become one.
I want to lift off with my load—
three-point-five billion passengers treading down their dead,
stamping on baby faces, clawing each other down—
out to where there's no ground, no sky, no air,
no voice, not even silence, anywhere.

Visiting Yeats's Tower

Flourish or not, my vocation is to be
the poet of a lifetime, as was he,
and range that lifetime against my fantasy—
my poor knowledge against my threadbare belief.
I too must riddle, "Perfection of the life,
or of the work?"—must find my tower, bring my wife
and children up round the stairway, for all to see
them cower on the battlement with me.

A clown's hubris, to mask the naked face
with a still more naked, vulnerable grimace,
mimic the spiralings of our spinning race
with a sweaty bourgeois climb, and, at tower-top poised,
wheeze through a tickling throat: "Life? Work? My voice
cracks and wobbles, yet Song is my only choice!"
Resonant, impenetrable still, that place
we'd thought to reach, reality's sheer grace.

Reality is here, green, drowsy, around
Yeats's old pretentious tower, and the sound
of his leaping stream out-sings what my musings found.
Ballylee's here; and there, a mile off, lived
the Gregories. When troopers came by, Yeats grieved
that he could but dream what less brooding men achieved:
passionate action, that holds life and work spellbound—
real, murderous, even on this provincial ground.

Memory: A Meditation and a Quarrel with the Master

"I died
before you could remember me again."

So a voice, in a dream itself hardly remembered . . .

We can't get past Hamlet's questions, or even Hardy's.
Please forgive me. These heaps of human skulls (each
held eternity at bay, until eternity became
at one with mortality) do trouble my imagination sorely.
I quarrel with the master's beloved words. Man never "created death."

My argument a friend's battered Irish face, his smiling skull,
cracked on a stone when he dived in an unknown stream,
abandoning his hornrimmed battlements. Oh, well I know
his body was not bruised to pleasure Tom. There's no place
outside our skulls for that kind embittered face to live;
or that other's round, Roman face, great-eyed as Juno's . . .

Merely friends' faces. Little history knows or cares.
I marshall those faces, call them back, bid them speak.
I alone remember them as I remember them.

I teach in the long classroom, questioning. The students,
burning or remote, reply or wait. Words that Tom and I, Henry and I,
held dear together, saying them with love, flow through the room
catching this soul or that into a kind of flame or light:

youthful recognition that pain and gaiety are one.
"The swan has leaped into the desolate heaven." Where's the old man
whose lunch I brought him daily, our boarder shivering
in his small watchman's shack, the oily smoke
from his kerosene stove scalding my baby nostrils?
Where's my young stepfather I'd meet at the trolley station,
stumbling through snowstorms with his galoshes when he came home from
work?
Where are the textile strikers raising high their picket signs
through the long winter days of 1928? Where's their leader Weisbord?
and the dream of the Union,
the songbursts of rage thrilling my childish heart?

Scattered
over wide America, the bones of men and women I loved
make one reply: "*We died*
before you could remember us again."

I stare at the sky
that glows as beautiful, as cold, as true to solitude
as when my mother walked upon the earth and dreamed
of how, when a girl, she'd dreamed
of returning home to Jónava to tell the peasants:
"Love one another, and the Jews, and lovely books and thoughts."

She: A Sequence of Poems

(1977)

In times to come,
it may be,
it will please us
to remember these things.

Tonight the stars are close.
They glitter so fiercely down
everything she says and is
points the long arrow toward my heart.
I'll lay me down
on early April's sparse, cold grass
and stare up through the cirrus clouds
into her clear heaven-wells
each with its naked glittering star.
It is the naked constellation, She,
and bends her glittering bow,
each arrow true to its mark.

She

She writes of sunburnt thighs,
a terrace of stone lions,
and Naxos just visible from her window.

This poor vessel, I,
one-oared, rudderless, droops
or, randy, unspent, shivers
in the moist night
towards gardens blowing where she sleeps or wakes. Dawn
is breaking there. And at its eastern gate
erratic trumpets blast their notes of war.
I'll beat into the wind as best I can.

Tack and turn as we will
close to or before the wind
whatever beats in the blood
can never be forgone.

I have been imagining
a small girl staring
through flawed crystal
at bombed babies, keening mothers.

Where gulls swoop for offal flung from freighters
and Oceanides flash their pearls of spray,
the thought of losing you washes over me again,
then sweeps back, away into the great sea.

There's
where the hawk must hang, sea-garden grow, battered pinnace
ride the abyss, sinking and rising, so.

Riddle of the Swan

Once, beating through the air, you amazed us.
We smiled under your shadow.

Broken-winged and raucous now, you're borne
whithersoever the torrent lists.

She and I, flung high on that arc where you made your song, never
before saw
our joined shadows beating and riding the torrent below.

We Begin These Things Lightly

We begin these affairs lightly
with an obscure smile, or an unseeing glance.

The soul, flung like rags on a greasy floor,
wavers into oneness again, tiny flames flickering.

Ecstasy

No more, then, to wander talking
into the querulous, misty, intimate hills?
Have you strayed too far from the others?
Do you shy away now, angry and anxious?

Still, after all, it's here—
a forgetting, not a death.
A hand touches, a banner flutters.
Over us, now, something waits and watches.

From a Distance

Miles off
you have your separate day.
Perhaps you lightly carry
my yesterday's body, memory's mannequin,
within yourself as I
drift in yours — cohabitants
of one another's quickened space.

It's here, though, everything unravels
in broad daylight, no place to go.
Gossamer tightropes dwindling to pollen.
Heart pounding as day and night converge.

Mule-kick of heart and brain, getting too excited.
I've got to get myself under control.
Something like a clear chime just to hold steady,
clean winter lines, a bright day just like this,
nothing disastrous, just remote, cool as your warm, absent kiss.

Imagining You Leaving Tangier Before a Storm

A wind blowing in Tangier. And you leaving, "heavy with luggage."
Hard to dismiss you from the mind's retina and let you be
one hustled mite in the mob scattered by the whimsy
of a Moroccan wind all but into the harbor. The dock-loungers
stare "Tourist-with-Frightened Eyes" at you. You're blown scurrying
onto the ship. And the old passengers, coming off, are hit
by the gusty darkness that lifts you so passionately
to ride on the swart seething seas. O, brave exchange!

I'm swept off the ship into black Tangier. The rain
finds me naked in its soaking chill. Coughing, my wallet already stolen,
I'm stripped by mumbling beggars, booked by the port police,
and hanged at dawn. And you, have you reached Algeciras yet?

First Time-Song

If I am very still, I may not be able to tell
how painfully the earth, shriek though it may through space,
turns. and turns. and turns. and turns. and creaks
on its rusted axletree. and creaks. until it stops
entirely. God! let me off
until the thing's cranked up again, and time
begins, again, to slip away so fast
it blisters everything that clings to it.

Second Time-Song

The hours inch by, the days yield not at all.
The steady weeks hold stoutly at their posts.

All day the honking cars and hooting boats
stream their hard designs of north and south.

Can I dream myself into oblivion?
If I rest my forehead on this hard old desk?

The clocks may race, the calendar's on strike.
Who shall roll this heavy time up and over the hill?

Compleynte, Etc

I cannot wait another day, and another day, yet do.
The waste of golden time clings to my fingers.
We're so ringed round with absence I can hardly move
toward you without a sudden leap of prayer.

Yet that famous golden laughter of the gods
invades me, amid these slipping days and nights,
these maelstroms, balked dreams, balancings
on snarling walls. Oh, two cosmic, comic acrobats

have swung from the bright hooked tips of the crescent moon
clasping, unclasping among the bristling hours
with a *ha-ha-ha* and a *hey, nonny-no*
and cries of *Impetuous Pistil!* and *Ah! sweet Stamen!*

Intimacy

With flagrant fingers
I fling wide the window
upon our opened world.

How intimate our world
with all the loving
man-and-woman smells.

Did you think I didn't love
the smell of you?
Idiot!

Not that the four blackbirds
screeching and scooting past
are intimate with us, not that they give a damn.

Ah but this opened world
is intimate with them
whether they give a damn or not.

By My Troth

I want
   nothing dearer
   than what I await
   with believing, unbelieving heart
   day by day.

I think
   of you moving
   in rooms far from me.
   The telephone! the postman!
   I'll shower them with kisses.

I know
   we are not one.
   Other lives and loves
   in rooms far from me
   have possessed you.

I have
   found you —
   death to the contrary.
   If our souls are ships
   adrift on the same sea,
   I want nothing dearer.

Fable of the Mermaid and the Drunks

All these guys were inside there
when she came in the door completely naked
they were drunk they started spitting at her
she didn't understand she'd just come up out of the river
she was only a mermaid who'd lost her way
their insults splattered her bright flesh
their obscenities smeared her breasts of gold
she didn't know about crying she didn't cry
she didn't know about dressing she had no clothes on
they stubbed out their cigarettes on her and marked her up with burnt cork
they laughed so hard they were rolling on the tavern floor
she didn't say anything she didn't know about talking
her eyes were the color of far-off love
her arms were made of matching topazes
her lips moved silently in a coral light
at last she left by that same door
she'd hardly plunged back in the river when she was clean again
shining like a white stone in the rain again
and without looking back she swam off once more
swam off to the void swam off to die

from the Spanish of Pablo Neruda

Long Night

Between the dark and the daylight
longing that mutes itself to the tick of the drifting minutes
these weary dreams on the seas of others' sleep
one-tick-and-then-another and the eyes neither closed nor open
Who so list to hount I know beyond the Alps
where is an hynde lies Italy   She opes to the searching touch
of these drifting fingers of dream her warm turning
sole self bright with her white marvels her eyes
of night her remembering thoughts her waking
portals of delight   And the long night narrows
to an hour's sleep just after dawn.

I Know Where Is an Hynde

The doe and her three fawns have returned.
They've crossed the hurtling highway from the mountain
just for crab apples, or our delight.
If we approach they freeze, and then
westward into one wood flies the doe,
eastward, into the other, the three fawns go.

Strange how some acid of the mind
burns away the bruise of days
yet leaves this glow of our delight.
And we here now, talking and caressing,
know love holds steady, that began before we knew,
though fawn must run at last where doe cannot pursue.

These autumn woods blaze up for our delight.
These leaves are fire
that love kindled, in forgotten other seasons.
Follow the doe's trail back up the mountain
to our own voices glowing in the mist — both she
and we flame there, fed by all memory.

Over and over I've thought never to forget
even the tiniest broken creature by the highway,
yet hardly remember souls I've clambered after
fanatical, will-o'-the-wisps on the trail of our delight.
The doe and her fawns feed under the crab apple tree.
Dear love, we know how sweet their breaths must be.

Incantation

First, to say your name aloud. Then, touch your cheek.
Then, stretch my whole length of self against
the warm length of you and hold you, thus, until
yet once more, again, the loaves and fishes multiply.

I say your name aloud. I touch your cheek.
I stretch my whole length of self against
the warm length of you and hold you, thus, until,
yet once more, again, the loaves and fishes multiply.

Slash of sea-wind. Stab of wild-rose thorn.
Violent heaped sunlight of our days.
Harshness of your love-gasp. Glittering circlet of your name.

Once

"Mistress," I said to her
whose name is body of my desire,
"will these green days
remain with us forever?"

"Mistress," I said to her
whose name is all my thought,
"I had forgot
the very name of Death.
Desire for Her blew through me once like the mistral."

A cold, forgotten voice replied,
"Desire blew through us once like the mistral."

Second Rilke Variation
("Einmal, wenn ich dich verlier")

Some day, when I lose you,
clear as, real as, today,
will we think, *This is the very day,*
Golden and blue, that's the last day?

When space and time, for once, hold firm,
never to return upon themselves,
will we two, touching and listening,
think to think, *This day leaves no shadow?*

Will we feel only the usual desolation
settling on us until . . . the next time?
Or will we think, *But this day stands alone?*
This is the day that, for once, has no end?

Bequest

Burn our sweet story,
let the wind carry its smoke away.
Hasten, hasten —
leave no shred to betray
our names, where we went, why we lingered,
whom we loved, when we wept, on what day.

Albatross

Near the Wailing Wall

an old woman in the sun

              head hanging

Not Quite Metaphysical

Is this the real you, then?
Or is it the real you of my imagination, then?
And shall I trouble myself about which is which?

A man doesn't want to be a fool,
at least not the kind of fool
he doesn't want to be

in the ironical eye
of a sensible woman
who keeps her own sensible counsel.

The Darkest Dream

I used this word, "joy,"
as my argument.
But misery lacks words —
there's no debate.

I used it, next,
as my talisman.
But misery is blind —
there's no remission.

And then, suddenly,
I could no longer say
it even to you —
so mute is misery.

Suddenly at the Edge

Suddenly at the edge, black ocean below,
and over the edge, flight without wings,
soughing of waves, stillness of star-pierced air,
tight-clenched and silent motion.

                  Soughing of leaves
now in my memory
holds, like your smile flickering towards me,
buoyant tracers ablaze, as when you
woke lovely and drowsy and lay down beside me
and we played like dolphins, awash in the night.

Night Vision (1973)

What is this bitter taste — your long absence.
Glistening berries sicken on the vine.

Candle-dim, across light-years,
your white shoulder rising above my head,

and, above the stilled kingdoms of glittering days,
the trees of night looming from forgotten graves.

Cold flash of light among the unmoving shades:
fireflies flicker against the tree-trunks.

Crack of a bullet in the silent street
and the skull, shattered, too heavy with history.

Young killers thunder over ancient villages.
Crackling flesh replies to the tongues of flames.

Saint

Eternal
"You,"
bless me among
Your other phalloi.

If I am gentle
do not think me
less fierce
than You.

So many
crimson with pride
do not know
I am proud too.

This calling dust,
under the sky's
blazing clock:
"I."

Joy

From some cold place in the great wobbling chaos
we have entered each other's forests and skies.

You are there. I see you when I dare to look.
Somewhere, once, was the place
where I knew this arrival must some day be so.

Waves of all force enter us from all that surrounds us.
Our hearts are beating steady as we wander
out of all space into each other's forests and skies.

Now I stand upright within your deepest, greenest glade
here, where we speak of plainest, most needful things.
Around me, above me, your face, your voice, holding steady.

Through Streets Where Smiling Children

Sometimes, out of your woman world,
your other memories, times, spaces, faces,
the chill of otherness blows across
our grove. You say a truth that's of
yourself, not us. My sloe-eyed darling, nobody's rich
as you. You
want me to speak how we are, and your own clear voice
rises up out of me, the other I
in its other sphere, making things clear,
sorting us out. Lying here, caressed,
caressing your breasts, the swell of your thighs,
marvelous plains of your flanks where armies of kisses march,
roused by the honeydew of your murmuring mouth,
I'll bring charges in no court of law against
your otherness. You are. And I have seen, too,
the chill of steel beams — no, the high oaks,
distant, unto themselves, of your quick thought's slow flourishing.

Say your television cops and cries of "Bullshit!"
cut across our dreams like iodine splashes.
Cafés in Paris, the Luxembourg Gardens, hand-to-mouth romance
on the run till I expire of ecstasy in some sweaty garret
while you, Eve Curie, go on to glory
wearing my poems between your perfumed breasts —

Bullshit. Begin again, then,
something that will work, a plainer plan. Still,
we improvise it all out of bits and pieces, dream-shards.
Everything you've dreamt has brought me to this grove, and you to me.
Everything I've dreamt too.

You have gathered the violence of your heart
into ordered days and places. Sunlight bathes you
in wavering lines, near tiny tropical fish
whose fins shimmer in luminous green amid
the bubbles streaming and bursting about them.
You wear your passion lightly, like a summer frock,
through streets where smiling children kick
each other's heads, twist each other's penises,
past hallways where broken beings retch unheard,
where blood drips from women cowed by unseen fists.
(Perhaps he will finish her off with switchblade and prick,
some slum Don Giovanni, proud killer and lover,
seizing her breasts for his instant of triumph, his accolade her
                                        paralyzed scream.)
You have gathered the violence of your heart's need
into clear spaces for the soul's ordering: your mind
at the ready, wearing your life lightly,
as the trees outside your window keep thrusting upward, "lightly."

You think you are alone. The sunlight comes in through your window
and finds you gravely at your desk or, poised among saucers,
manuscript, stove, and phonograph, juggling the long hours
with "so much to do." What is a "vision"? Your face, in laughter
or repose

shadow or light. Your self, very still or walking on a street,
or poured like nectar into a voice I drink from all hours.

For a Moment

— As if, after all, it has gone.
Defined, snapped shut, buried.

                    And all still alive back there,
the shades, the levels of green you loved. Still there.

Even a ghost has things, except to die, to do.

Did you ever imagine, as a child,
these silences falling away
from where death watched us for a moment
and then the mockingbird's manic medley
wild with the morning, wild for heaven to notice.

The Stranger, The Beloved

(New Poems)

Which of Us, Then, Will It Be

The river drowns our voices,
the huge bridge cows our thought.
The lights above the water
speak for all that's dead or mute.
Yet our hearts converse:
we are in such earnest!
We speak— no matter what we say.

It seems we are death-bound.
Which of us, then, will it be?
For one must die, says the river;
must die, say the bridge and the lights.
We are all so gravely agreed.
Though the heart be evergreen,
this is doom, was always here.

(The boy Chatterton, green in the painting.
The pretty little house.
A mist drops over the past,
over the innocent gravestone.
The boy Chatterton in velvet and silk.
The room where he wrote his poems.
Memory a green bruise.)

The lamp glows as in a drawing,
its rays streaming black lines.
Books, paper. Like an old life
the new life wells up. The
chair, the typewriter waiting.
The desk stands (*in medias res*!)
electric, disordered, alive.

The man in spectacles knows all:
swift, invisible, efficient,
has told me. Death's cast
down the long river
is what you chose, suddenly,
while I . . . he knows,
he will not say.

Time clamps down.
Chair, lamp.
A mist over the green bruise.
Turn back, irreversible moment.
Perfect dream, perfectly formed,
turn back.
Where is the innocent place?

The lights gleam up from the river.
He will never say.
Silent. Will never tell.
Raindrop-shadows inside the car-door;
the shadow of the wiper removes them.
Never to find your young grave.
Silent the bridge and the lights.

I awake! It is not true!
The morning is sweet with rain.
The long swift Thames of the mind
still floods over its banks.
Death's indelible bruise
blazes again on the desk. Thrice blessed:
the long cast was but for me.

To William Carlos Williams in Heaven

Your poems, earthy old ghost,
rise through the moon-troubled air.
Tonight they mock and remind
like old Caruso recordings.

The buses roar through the Jersey
meadows past your bones, poor Bill.
Ai mi madre—
Your burial day was sloppy and wet.

Far off, past the Pleiades . . .
Hell with all that!
In the starry depths, death . . .
So what!

In my hand an old book
where a boyish old voice
sings of love raped and mute
and a giant pissing into the river.

What turmoil! Your
workingclass Muse
led you *some* chase
right up the Bomb and the Holocaust—

till you caught her near the stinking Passaic
where you delivered all those babies
and lived with your nice tough wife,
your "small yellow sweet-scented violet"—

old lover with your "common" language!

God, of Course, Does Not Exist
(In memoriam Ramon Guthrie)

The man has spent a lifetime waiting for God, who does not exist.
God must appear, or must speak, in such a way as to reveal Himself
                                                        unmistakably.

And God—if He exists, but He doesn't—sees the man
waiting, yearning toward Him.

Oh, but perhaps God cannot make Himself visible?—He doesn't exist.
Or cannot understand what language means for men?—He doesn't exist.

But then the man dies. God, being non-existent, believes
the man has reached Him at last.

He smiles and says, in God-language,
I heard you. I saw you.

But now the man cannot see or hear.
God does not understand this.

Dannie's Grove

Because he died just after he put them in,
trailing his eighteenth year like a broken branch,
we call these trees he planted "Dannie's Grove."
The birds all love to wander or nest or hover here,
the crippled Canada goose and his friend the mallard
and a thousand comely civilians—robin, junco, cardinal, dove—
and wind-borne migrants pausing early and late
on the still-slender maples and tulips, budding again.
Dannie Murphy planted them here a year ago.
He said he'd replace the ones that didn't leaf and grow,
but all are doing fine again this spring.

June 1975

Farewell to Jeannie

I

Sexy old cradle-snatcher, earth, musky
seductress, with your swamp-wet grass-smells, your
white violets you drew us down to touch—
how you ravished us, old kidnapper! Your
green, soft slopes we rolled over, your lily-pads,
your pools, your spring-mud squelching underfoot—
how we loved your indifferent, secret tides . . .

II

Hard, fast, loose,
fallen where no sentimental breeze
heavy with summer breasts, country moist,
can promise love's clasp in the hedge
but mirroring shards sum up heaven and earth—
roadside bits of sky, car-bumpers, montage of rain and dust,
beercans and condoms, fragments of woodchuck:
death's found collage.

Season of raptors.
The hawks are moving.
I would send her
whatever she will,
this prayer if need be
against breath and blood.

III

Like remembered nights
on far-off boulevards
all we know for sure goes swaggering by
like a topless tart in tights
or Idi's bodyguards—
Do you know that lullaby?

Like a breath that sighs
"O Ulysses stay with me"
all we love for sure goes shimmering by
like a pair of perfect thighs
or the bankroll of Ali—
Do you know that lullaby?

Like a zero day
when peacocks puff their chests
all we are for sure goes shivering by
like a cold clench in love's play
or anything of Mae West's—
Do you know that lullaby?

Lines in Dejection

As I mount
the lush hillside

something crashes
in the brush

an owl shoots across my path

a doe freezes

Not even one elephant?
No madwomen screeching in the treetops?
Only three little portents and
such a fuss?

Postcard to Lord Byron (and You)

But tonight I did go a-roving
under that same full moon
I might have been far out at sea

on the cold billows of night
an idiot Jesus walking on light
hands, eyes, filled with moon's gold

winking at fireflies
and they winked back at me
for the night was made for loving, etc.

Though we spoke our love bravely
this night has come with a flashing of cold blades
fit foe to the firefly host—
Fireflies, man your glows!

This night I've gone a-roving
and seized my moon's-gold crown
I'm king of Firefly Town

for the night was once made for loving, etc.

In Praise of Sweet Chance

I

Thought lies clasped
within herself as, when
I "leave" you, our breaths
still mingle, our breasts
still pressing, our words
still clasped within
our remembering touch.

II

They cannot know the line
that bounds our grove
and so they come and go,
trampling our unseen shadows
thoughtlessly, carelessly,
as though we had never been.

III

Lucky this man (I) who, rising
out of dream-seas, already forgotten,
wakes into daylight thinking:
"There is a woman (you) who, rising,
now perhaps into daylight, may be thinking:
'Now perhaps he is waking.
Perhaps he is smiling, thinking of me:
"O worlds of delight that are yet to come." ' "

Bláck-cap Glád Song

("And smale foweles maken melodye")

When I hear the black-capped chickadee
    swéet call
    swéet fall
Aḱ well   aḱ me
think I hear you calling me
sómewhere   oút there
Aḱ well
    Got them cold weather blues
    Got that sense of desolation
                        —ólation
    Can't find my old elation
till I hear that bláck-cap
    Só sad   só glad
    Só glad   só sad
Aḱ well
    makes me feel só glad
when I hear the bláck-cap
    oút there
    sómewhere

Geometries of Manhattan : Morning

Foggy morning. The mist-held horizons
move closer, being broken now
by hulks without grace or thrust, not skyscrapers,
not experiments—dumped crates, deadweights
dropped by monsters on strike against the sun.
They block a mile of river, mile of sky.

                                 Still stately, serene,
the thwarted Hudson poises them in its frame
while, weary, soiled, the massed clouds brace them. The aching eye
presses, past clouds and water, to the ruined Jersey shore whose
mysterious, unfocused distances alone sustain
lost promises as mute as Leonardo's far-off forest green.

                                      And now
the relenting eye returns, the river brightens. One gull, two,
invite the dreamer back toward the wakening city. A raindrop-pool
ripples on a factory rooftop. A tiny cardboard carton
drifts from some crevice in the glittering heights,
a box-kite to the lucky watcher. Turning, turning,
past this hotel window, downward to older Manhattan
drifting and turning, towards the unseeing multitudes, the cars,
the shadows, the shafts of sunlight, the life below.

Listening, Watching

The illusion of the swan   was not
the swan   but

           the white drake
has a longer neck   than you might think

                 and
in the mist   arched it

      so.   And, conversely,

your frayed windbreak   old skirt   mudcaked shoes
on the road   not expected

            white swan at dusk
listening

One Afternoon

Lost to me again, and once again.
Green, hot, stormy, cold: shreds
of dried time spread on racks of wind;
like spring sun on new leaf,
never to be touched again.

Through shushing trees
from dazzled headwaters
pours the gold
splashing from branches:
pools of quick light
warm on dark lawn,
drowsy, their lovers awaiting,
woman-souls yearning
here, this hour, for
whoever will take them.

She is not lying there
curled in late sunlight
although she is there
and anywhere
our souls may choose.

Our love's book, leaves uncut:
oh, forgive my treasonous double thought—
 like a double rainbow, burning sign
 of all that blesses or is malign;
 the scream that spurts like blood, the pang
 of distant joy a solitary reaper sang—
the clasped book holds the imprint of it all.

Up the hill's path trudging, tracking
love. Two orioles at play
hide every face from me, as if
to say: even space and loss are filled
with wings flashing gold. My climb
done, you lie with me in the sun.
We reach down the long hillside
and gather the warm hours over us
before ever the foolish little furies return
to make us cold and alone again.

The Stranger, the Beloved

I

4 A.M., Barcelona, stark awake.
This narrow street all silent.
Even the smells, silent. All the clamoring ruck,
laughter slopping over windowsills, trucks revving,
Catalan caterwauling: dead. Thick-
dark milk-murky pre-dawn.
The air here's not to breathe. I alone, awake,
self-terrorist, visiting owl, keep watch.
Hard ring of footsteps down the obscene cobbles!

                                 From afar, afar

returning, in the wash of streets and years!

Down gutted street between storefront shutters
(washboard altars where gaunt laundresses pray)
hoofbeats of the arriver, thunder of terror,
army of one! No doorway to shrink in.

                                 Bursts into view

bag swung from shoulder, one beard with dark glasses
towards me, past, away.
And day breaks on the deconsecrated world.

II

So too it must be with the waiting dead.
I'll take my quiet place, lest one should come
thinking to find me, and find me gone.

Let me be watchful. Still.
A weathered slab of stone. Part of a wall.
Let dogs, drunks, drabs use me as they will.
Let me hold, steadfast, the narrowest space.

In fear, at dawn, I am yet the welcomer.
When you come with banners, thunder,
my shadowed eyes will open on the centuries.
You will ride the surging sea of masks.
You will not see my granite-gray welcomer's smile.

                                        No matter.

We are touched awake forever.

Notes

Blue Boy on Skates

"Three Conversations"—Jónava, usually spelled without an accent-mark, is a village in Lithuania.

Beyond Power

"A Dream of Mayakovsky's Suicide Note"—The one authentic quotation from Mayakovsky's suicide note here comes in the last line. He did not quote Mallarmé's "UN COUP DE DÉS."

The View from the Peacock's Tail

"Violence"—The terrible tidal waves that devastated East Pakistan (now Bangladesh) in the 1960s (and not only then) brought mass death, starvation, and very little help from elsewhere to that region of historical misery.

"Theater Talk," in its original form, was published as "Intermission."

"Geometries of Haifa: Night"—The barbed wire observed around beautiful garden-areas is a defensive measure, presumably.

*   *   *

About the Author

The lefthanded child of divorced parents,
What could he do but make
every triumph a mare's nest
and all delight a stammering mistake?

(But the next stanza, o my readers,
goes on, if it's ever written,
in a happier, altogether beautiful
and, certainly, affirmative vein.)

144

Index of Titles

Index of First Lines